Hi... My name is Parker and i'm here to take you through your daily affirmations!

Did you know that they help boost your confidence, improve mental health, relieves stress, build resilience, counter negativity, help to practise positivity, validate effort and acknowledge challenges?

As important as it is for parents to encourage, support and love our children, it is just as important that children learn to create this within themselves as well.

I have created 28 affirmation poems and pictures pages for you to read through each day.

HAVE FUN!!!

Daily Affirmations For Kids -28 Positive Rhyming Affirmation Poems For Kids And Toddlers | Poems For The Very Young

Cover by LHarris.
Ebook ISBN:

I AM thankful, I never give in, forever show gratitude, from under my skin.

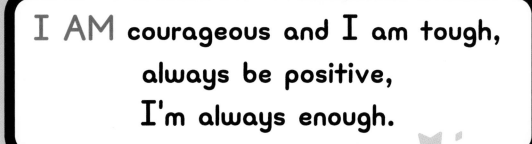

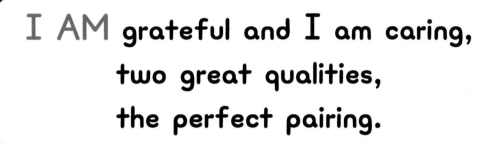

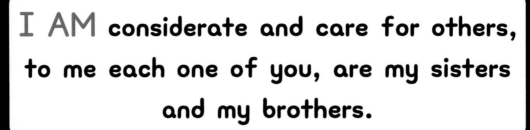

I AM considerate and care for others, to me each one of you, are my sisters and my brothers.

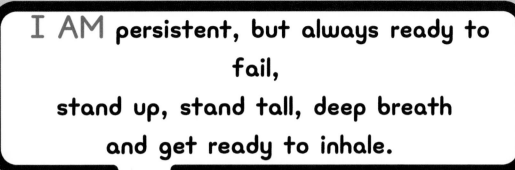

Printed in Great Britain
by Amazon